JEWISH BLOOD IS NO LONGER CHEAP

Alan Dershowitz Books Relating to the Jewish People, Israel, Terrorism, and the Laws of War

The Preventive State

Trump to Harvard: Go Fund Yourself

Palestinianism

The Ten Big Anti-Israel Lies

War Against the Jews

Defending Israel: The Story of My Relationship with My Most Challenging Client

The Case Against BDS: Why Singling Out Israel for Boycott Is Anti-Semitic and Anti-Peace

The Case Against the Iran Deal

The Case for Moral Clarity: Israel, Hamas and Gaza

The Case Against Israel's Enemies: Exposing Jimmy Carter and Others Who Stand in the Way of Peace

Pre-emption: A Knife That Cuts Both Ways

The Case for Peace: How the Arab-Israeli Conflict Can Be Resolved

The Case for Israel

Why Terrorism Works: Understanding the Threat, Responding to the Challenge

Chutzpah

The Best Defense

JEWISH BLOOD IS NO LONGER CHEAP

A Call to Arms in Preventing Recurrence of Past Disasters

ALAN DERSHOWITZ

PROFESSOR EMERITUS HARVARD LAW SCHOOL

Skyhorse Publishing

Skyhorse Publishing books may be purchased in bulk at special discounts for sales promotion, corporate gifts, fund-raising, or educational purposes. Special editions can also be created to specifications. For details, contact the Special Sales Department, Skyhorse Publishing, 307 West 36th Street, 11th Floor, New York, NY 10018 or info@skyhorsepublishing.com.

Skyhorse® and Skyhorse Publishing® are registered trademarks of Skyhorse Publishing, Inc.®, a Delaware corporation.

Visit our website at www.skyhorsepublishing.com.
Please follow our publisher Tony Lyons on Instagram @tonylyonsisuncertain.

10 9 8 7 6 5 4 3 2 1

Library of Congress Cataloging-in-Publication Data is available on file.

Paperback ISBN: 978-1-5107-8683-7
eBook ISBN: 978-1-5107-8684-4

Cover design by Brian Peterson

Printed in the United States of America

This book is lovingly dedicated in memory of my son Elon, who worked alongside me for more than half a century defending Jews, Israel, and values we both cherished. We traveled together to the Soviet Union, Western Europe, Egypt, China, Israel, the Palestinian Authority, and other locations on behalf of human rights. He made each of my books better, through his brilliant insights and edits. I will miss his love, kindness, support, and companionship every day of my life.

Contents

Introduction

The Talmud commands that if someone comes to kill you, "rise up and kill them first." Too often, however, Jews have failed to anticipate and rise up against those who were planning to kill them. We have also failed to demand just revenge and effective deterrence against those who have spilled Jewish blood. We cannot afford the doom of repetition. We must rise up now to prevent recurrence.

History rarely, if ever, repeats itself with exactitude, despite George Santayana's admonition that "those who cannot remember the past are condemned to repeat it." But failure to see parallels to past disasters and take preventive measures increases the likelihood of comparable horrors, currently or in the future. The dire, dangerous trajectories facing Jews and their nation-state Israel mandate a keen focus on the experiences and failures of German Jews from 1932 to 1945. There are those who would like to see a repetition of the Holocaust, not only Iranian mullahs and Hamas terrorists, but some radical students around the world. We cannot afford to ignore these haters.

Let me begin with a disclaimer: Although there are some striking parallels between current events and past ones, I do not believe that we will ever again experience anything like the Holocaust, which resulted in the murder of six million Jews. The world is a different place today than it was back then. Most importantly, the

Jewish people and Israel are far stronger and more able to fight proactively and reactively than they were in the lead-up to the Holocaust. This strength was evidenced by Israeli's overwhelming responses to the pogrom of October 7. Although some deem these responses "disproportional," they resulted in the release of all remaining live hostages—and with the help of the United States, the destruction of much of Iran's nuclear weapons program as well as the capacity of its surrogates to wage war against Israel. That is not to say that Jews and their state do not face grave dangers from growing antisemitism, anti-Zionism, and the application of a negative double standard to all things Jewish. They most certainly do, even if not to the degree experienced by their predecessors. We must remember the past, learn from it, and commit to never tolerating anything even close to the disasters that befell the Jewish people between 1939 and 1945, and on October 7.

In order to assure "never again," the Jewish people must undertake preventative and preemptive measures and not rely only on reacting to clear and present dangers. That was the critical misstep of the 1930s, when we underestimated the tragedy that awaited the Jewish people until it was too late to stop it. We must learn the lesson of that tragic miscalculation, try hard to anticipate the future, and act to influence it in real time. In doing so, we may make mistakes, but the mistake of underreacting must be avoided even at the risk of overreacting. That is one of the most important lessons of the 1930s, when the Jewish leadership tragically underreacted for fear of being accused of overreacting to what should have been obvious dangers. There are numerous tragic examples of such fear of offending non-Jewish leaders by prominent leaders such as Justice Felix Frankfurter, Rabbi Stephen Wise, Arthur Ochs Sulzberger, and other well-situated Jews who had the ears of presidents, prime ministers, the media, academia, business leaders, and other influencers but refused to act out of fear of offending or being accused of "crying wolf." "*Sha-shtill*"—be quiet—was a common reflection of the ghetto mentality that still prevailed in many Jewish quarters. The title of a recent biography by Rafael Medoff of Rabbi Wise summarized the situation with a direction by President Theodore Roosevelt to Wise: "The Jews should keep quiet," and Roosevelt's insistence—even in the early 1940s—that it was "too early to intervene." In my 1991 book *Chutzpah*, I assessed the situation as I then saw it:

> American Jews need more Chutzpah. Notwithstanding the stereotype, we are not pushy or assertive enough for our own good and for the good of our more vulnerable brothers and sisters in other parts of the world. Despite our apparent success, deep down we see ourselves as second class citizens—as guests in other people's land. We worry about charges of dual loyalty, of being too rich, too smart, and too powerful. Our cautious leaders obsess about what the 'real' Americans will think of us.

I also predicted back then that "we will continue to witness a sharp decline in support for Israel among college and university students," who will become "tomorrow's leaders." I predicted that "unless this trend can be reversed, it bodes ill for the long-term interests of Israel." Unfortunately, this prediction has turned out to be true, and the interest of Israel and the Jewish community face even greater dangers now than they did thirty-five years ago. We must take steps, even risky ones, to try to reverse these trends and reduce the dangers.

Striking an appropriate balance is desirable, but the crucial lesson of our history is that if mistakes are inevitable, and they generally are, it is better—or at least less worse—to err on the side of overreacting than underreacting to impending existential threats.

A. Overreacting to the October 7 Massacres Was Demanded by the History of Underreacting to Jewish Bloodletting

Israel's military actions following the massacres of October 7, 2023, were a historical reaction to centuries of underreaction. For thousands of years, Jews have been the victims of pogroms and racist violence culminating in, but not ending with, the Holocaust. The murderers rarely paid for their actions. Jewish blood was cheap. Even most perpetrators of the Holocaust were never brought to justice. Many hands-on mass murderers lived good lives in a postwar Germany that was quickly rebuilt by the Marshall Plan. Hitler assured the German people that if they got rid of the Jews, they would be better off economically. The Marshall Plan, which was made necessary by Soviet competition, rewarded Germany for spilling so much Jewish blood.

For decades, the Palestinian Authority gave so-called welfare payments to terrorists who had killed Jews—the "pay for slay" policy. Those who died killing Jews were considered martyrs and their families compensated. Many of their leaders—those who planned the killings—lived in the luxury of Qatar and other locations that provided gilded sanctuaries. The murderers and rapists who participated in the October 7 massacre seemed to think they'd get away with it. They took videos of the atrocities they committed and bragged about killing Jews wherever they could find them. And indeed, with the release of Palestinian prisoners who participated in the October 7 terrorist attack, some did get away with it.

But this time it was different, for the most part. Israel fought back and made many of the perpetrators and their supporters pay a heavy price. Some believe the price has been too heavy, especially for innocent civilians in Gaza. We don't know the precise number of completely innocent victims. Gaza's Health Ministry, run by Hamas, doesn't distinguish between civilians and combatants when it claims that more than sixty thousand Gazans have been killed since October 7, 2023. There are good reasons to doubt that figure and even better reasons to doubt the absurd claim that fewer than ten thousand of them were combatants. The criteria for categorizing someone as a combatant aren't black and white, especially in a war waged by terrorist groups. There is a continuum from combatant to civilian.

On the clear end of the combatant side are the terrorists themselves: members of Hamas, Islamic Jihad, and other designated terrorist groups. But there are also "civilians" who were complicit in the October 7 massacre by crossing into Israel and participating directly in the murders, rapes, and kidnappings. Many more joined forces with Hamas by hiding rocket launchers in their homes, holding Israeli hostages, digging and supplying the terror tunnels, and engaging in other activities that make them combatants in the moral sense if not in the strictly legal sense.

Consider, for example, the family of Mahmoud Afana, who was a member of the Hamas Nukhba force. On October 7, he murdered several Israeli civilians, including a husband and wife, in Kibbutz Mefalsim. He then took the wife's phone and called his parents in Gaza. He bragged that he was "talking to you from a Jewish woman's phone. I killed her and her husband with my own hands. Open your WhatsApp and look at all the killed. Look at how many I killed with my own hands. Your son killed Jews. . . . Mom, your son is a hero." He then boasted that he had murdered ten Jews with his own hands. The mother responded: "wish I was there with you." According to reports by Arab speakers who listened to the recording, the father "could be heard in the audio crying tears of joy." Afana also told his brother that the blood of ten Jews "is on my hands."

Nearly two years after these cold-blooded murders, Afana himself was killed by an Israeli air strike. He was certainly a combatant who deserved his fate as a matter of law and morality. But what about his adult family members who cheered him on and encouraged him? Are they "innocent" civilians, as a matter of morality, if not law? We do not know their fate, but if they suffered collateral death or injury as a consequence of a legitimate IDF military operation, would a moral person be wrong for not shedding tears of woe for the father of a murderer who himself shed tears of joy for the murder of ten innocent Jews? Or for the mother of a murderer who wished she were at the scene of the murders? Where do these supporters of terror lie along the continuum of pure innocence to moral complicity? Nor were they the only "innocent" civilians who cheered for the terrorists and actively welcomed the massacres. Many, if not most, Gazans approved the massacres, rapes, and kidnappings of October 7. Do they not share at least some moral complicity? There is no simple black and white answer to this and other questions of degree. And what if Afana had been seventeen years old, or a woman, when he murdered ten innocent Jews?

Although the Gaza Health Ministry doesn't distinguish between combatants and civilians, it does distinguish men from women and children. By listing them separately, the organization seeks to imply that women and children cannot be terrorists. But they often are—and they kill Jews as surely as other combatants do. Many combatants are women, and many are fifteen-, sixteen- and seventeen-year-olds who fire rockets and shoot guns. They should not be listed separately in order to imply a lesser degree of complicity. Even when listed separately by age, the largest number of "children" noted as killed were sixteen and seventeen years old, with many of them likely to be combatants.

The number of truly innocent civilians who have been killed by Israel is certainly far lower than the figures featured in much of the media. The sixty thousand–plus figure includes Gazans killed accidently by terrorist rockets, as well as those murdered deliberately by Hamas gunmen. Whatever the actual death toll among innocent children and other actual civilians, it is too high, as a matter of morality and emotion. But Hamas must bear responsibility for most of these deaths as well, because Hamas started the war and because it uses schools, hospitals, mosques, and other civilian structures to hide combatants.

After Israel suffered the worst massacre of Jews since the Holocaust, it sent a powerful and long overdue message of deterrence to those who perpetrated and supported the mass killing. Jewish blood is no longer cheap and those who shed it will pay a heavy, even disproportionately heavy price, so as to avoid recurrence. Although Israel didn't target innocent civilians, it took extraordinary measures to kill every terrorist it could who had participated in the atrocities of October 7—as well as their leaders. Israel inevitably caused considerable collateral damage, namely killing innocent civilians who were in or around military targets, despite its efforts to minimize such casualties. Hamas welcomed the deaths of Gazan civilians, knowing that these deaths would hurt Israel in the court of public opinion. The media played into Hamas's hands by featuring casualties without context, and without comparing the ratio of civilians to combatant deaths in other comparable wars.

It's unclear whether the Israeli policy will deter future massacres, because Hamas brags that it loves death as the Israelis love life. What is a democracy to do when its terrorist enemies threaten to repeat the atrocities of October 7 over and over again? And when its leaders are not deterred by the collateral deaths of their followers?

Winston Churchill recognized that strategic bombing of German towns and cities was necessary in some instances to stop Nazi aggression. Franklin Roosevelt agreed. Harry S. Truman took a similar approach when he ordered the atomic bombing of Hiroshima and Nagasaki, recognizing that civilian casualties would be necessary to deter the Japanese from further aggression. An important effect of the bombings, even if not the sole purpose, was to demoralize the population and turn them against their leaders. History has generally not condemned the Allies for their successful strategy in ending the war, though most of the civilian deaths they caused were intended rather than collateral. Yet Israel is being disproportionately condemned despite its extraordinary efforts to reduce civilian casualties, and its far better ratio of civilian to combatant deaths.

Israel must treat Hamas and Islamic Jihad the way the Allies treated the Nazis and the imperial Japanese. These terrorists must be totally defeated, and only then should their cities be rebuilt, as German and Japanese cities were. Just as peace would not have been possible in 1945 if the Nazis and imperialists were allowed to survive and remain in control, so too Hamas and Islamic Jihad must not be allowed to survive.

European countries, the United Nations, the mainstream media, academics, and the Left will all condemn Israel if it continues to defend itself against Hamas. But the message Israel has sent to the world—that Jewish blood is no longer cheap, and those who shed it will pay a heavy price—is a historical imperative, even if it is seen as a necessary evil. It is long overdue and was made essential by centuries of people around the world tolerating the shedding of Jewish blood without consequence. Morality is not an abstract or theoretical concept. It must be informed by experience, history, and reality. With these considerations in mind, Israel's reaction to the brutalities of October 7 must be deemed moral.

B. Even If It Was an Overreaction, Israel's Military Actions Were Not Even Close to Genocide

It has become fashionable among anti-Israel zealots—including hard-left academics—to use the term "genocide" to characterize Israel's response to the murder, rape, beheadings, and kidnapping of more than 1,450 innocent Israelis on October 7, 2023.

Self-proclaimed "genocide scholar" Omer Bartov wrote in *The New York Times* that he knows genocide when he sees it, and he sees it in Gaza, though not in Israel on October 7. A self-proclaimed association of Holocaust scholars (anyone can join for $30) voted to accuse Israel of genocide. The king of Jordan accused Israel of genocide following the lead of the biased UN rapporteur on Palestine. Others followed.

The label will no doubt be a central part of campus rallies and UN condemnations.

But this accusation is false as a matter of fact, morality, logic, and law—and a dangerous distortion of history that amounts to Holocaust denial. It trivializes the powerful term "genocide" and applies it to nearly every war fought by democracies during the last century, especially those directed against terrorism and other forms of modern asymmetrical warfare. By doing so, it encourages terrorism and emboldens terrorists who use civilian human shields to force their enemies into making tragic and deadly choices. Most distressingly, it makes genocide a meaningless epithet to be tossed around promiscuously by those opposed to particular wars or nations.

The Holocaust was the personification of genocide. Its expressed aim was the destruction of the entire Jewish race, wherever they could be located. The Nazis imported Jews—every Jew or partial Jew they could find, babies, the elderly, pregnant women, Catholic priests and nuns with a Jewish grandparent—from distant locations in order to gas them.

Not only did the systematic mass murder of six million Jewish civilians serve no military purpose, on many occasions the Nazis actually compromised military goals to accomplish their non-military goal of murdering every baby who had a Jewish genetic forebearer.

They went so far as to ingather Jews from areas that were not even military targets and transfer them to death camps. These willful and systematic efforts to exterminate an entire "race" is what geno-cide is. And it bears absolutely no relationship to what Israel has done to Gaza: Every civilian death in Gaza is collateral to achieving legitimate military goals. Every civilian has been told to leave or move to safer areas so that the IDF can target only combatants.

Even those who believe that Israel has gone too far in collater-ally killing a disproportionate number of Palestinian civilians must acknowledge that Israeli actions do not parallel the gas chambers, mobile killing units, and ingatherings that characterized the Nazi genocide.

To compare these two very different efforts is to suggest one of two possible conclusions: Either the Nazis did not employ gas chambers and other systematic methods of deliberately murder-ing every Jew they could find; or the Israeli government's military campaign is morally indistinguishable from the Nazi death camps. Neither is credible, but that does not seem to matter to anti-Israel zealots who do not care about facts or truth.

What Israel is doing is in no way comparable to the genocide planned and implemented at the Wannsee Conference of 1942. It may be comparable, though not in degree, to the hundreds of thou-sands of civilian deaths caused by American and British military actions following D-Day—including firebombing Dresden, Berlin, and Tokyo and dropping atomic bombs on Hiroshima and Nagasaki. These military attacks were designed to destroy Nazism, defeat the armies that had started World War II, and prevent a recurrence— just as Israel's actions in Gaza are designed to destroy Hamas and prevent a recurrence of October 7. If anything, the Allied bombings were worse: they were not directed primarily at important military targets, but at innocent civilian populations in an effort to demor-alize them and to get them to demand surrender.

The number and proportion of civilian casualties in those Allied operations well exceeded even the exaggerated numbers provided by the Hamas health authorities. In other words, accusing Israel of genocide in Gaza constitutes a false claim that the United States and its allies did practice it too, in their heroic battle to defeat Nazi Germany and Imperial Japan. It accuses our "greatest generation" of the worst crime known to humanity. It also accuses other nations that have waged wars since the end of World War II. Although the term "genocide"—the mass murder of an entire race or ethnicity—was not coined until after World War II, the crime of targeting civilian population centers was well recognized by the laws of war. We may still compare and contrast what Israel is doing now to what the Allies did then. Any such comparison favors Israel.

Consider the ratio of civilian to combatant deaths, which is lower for Israel than for any army facing comparable enemies— especially those using civilians as human shields to protect their combatants. Even if Hamas's phony figures are considered, the ratio of civilian to combatant deaths in the Gaza War is considerably less than half the ratio in other comparable wars.

In addition to bragging about using civilians as martyrs, Hamas hides its terrorists in protected tunnels while requiring civilians to remain above ground and vulnerable to military attack.

Israel gains nothing and loses much whenever it kills a civilian in the course of trying to neutralize terrorists—but Hamas gains sympathy every time Israel accidentally kills a civilian, especially a child.

That is the Hamas strategy, and those who falsely accuse Israel of genocide incentivize the continuing use of this murderous gambit. Regardless of the lies disseminated by phony "scholars," Israel has not come close to committing genocide. Anyone who claims they have deserves no credibility as an expert, scholar, or commentator. They are either knaves or fools, probably both.

C. Moving People in Order to Secure Peace Is Not Genocide

Nations intent on committing genocide do not give their intended targets an opportunity to leave and save their lives. If the Jews of Germany, Poland, Ukraine, Hungary, and other genocidal murder locations had been offered an opportunity to move or be moved to safe areas, there would have been no genocide or Holocaust. Most, including many of my relatives, wanted nothing more than to move, but they were trapped and murdered. It is ironic therefore for the United States and Israel to be accused of war crimes for proposing that Gazan civilians be given the option of moving from war zones to safe countries or areas. History teaches us that relocation of people is sometimes necessary to secure an enduring peace. Ethnic Germans had lived in Sudetenland for generations. Their presence there played a significant role in the Nazi aggression against Czechoslovakia that led to World War II. After the defeat of Germany, millions of ethnic Germans were relocated out of Sudetenland. This helped bring about enduring peace in Central Europe.

Similarly, the relocation of many Indian and Pakistani residents after the end of British colonial rule helped stabilize that area.

Wars result in population movements, especially for residents of nations that initiated the wars, such as Germany that lost the Königsberg area to the Soviet Union after World War II. When the Soviet Union defeated Germany, it transferred nearly the entire German population of Königsberg, renamed it Kaliningrad, repopulated it with ethnic Russians, and annexed it to the Soviet Union, which was hundreds of miles away.

World leaders, including Winston Churchill and President Harry Truman, deemed these population transfers necessary. They were not without serious difficulties, including the deaths of some innocent people, but history has demonstrated that they were worth the cost.

Peace is more important than place, and if an enduring peace in the Middle East could be achieved with temporary or even longer-term population transfers, then it is an option worth considering. Deploying loaded terms such as "ethnic cleansing" and "population transfers" does not solve what has long appeared to be the intractable problems associated with the Gaza Strip, which was originally part of Egypt, then occupied by Israel, then returned to Palestinian control, and subsequently taken over in a coup by the terrorists of Hamas.

The ultimate goal of a completely rebuilt, demilitarized "Singapore on the Mediterranean" will not be easy to achieve. But it may be worth trying. Peaceful Arab and Muslim nations could temporarily take over portions of the Gaza Strip, destroy the terrorist tunnels underneath the land, and rebuild it in a way that minimizes the prospects of remilitarization by Hamas. Palestinian families could then be returned to the rebuilt areas after being vetted to exclude Hamas terrorists and supporters. This will not be easy, but neither would any other solution to the Gaza problem.

Palestinian residents of areas subject to reconstruction could be generously compensated for their dislocation by funds provided by wealthy Arab states in the region. It is inevitable, however, that some Palestinian residents of Gaza will refuse to move, even temporarily, for fear that they will never be allowed to return. It is also likely that Hamas would threaten any residents who accepted payment to move. Accordingly, some degree of compulsion would be necessary as it was in Sudetenland, India, Pakistan, and Königsberg. When it comes to peace in Gaza, there are no free lunches—only the comparative costs of imperfect actions versus disastrous nonactions.

A demilitarized Gaza would dramatically increase the chances of a broader resolution to the Israel-Palestinian conflict. It would open the door to new ideas about the governance of the West Bank. It might encourage the Arab states, especially Saudi Arabia, to join the Abraham Accords. A return to the status quo, with Gaza remaining under the control of terrorist groups and rebuilding its tunnels, holds no similar prospects for an enduring peace.

There is no perfect solution. Every plan will have its pitfall, every idea its detractors, and every alternative its downside. But in considering the options, history must be kept in mind. And historical precedents show that moving populations—by choice or even by force—is often the least worst alternative and has frequently contributed to peace.

D. The Excruciating Dilemma Faced by a Moral Democracy That Must Retrieve Hostages While Defeating Its Terrorist Enemies

Democracies at war have long needed to confront the dilemma of fighting their enemies without killing their own soldiers who have been captured and deliberately put in harm's way. The US and Great Britain killed a considerable number of their own captured soldiers when they bombed German and Japanese military targets that held allied POWs. They were aware of the risks that captives could be killed by friendly fire, but they balanced those unavoidable risks against the military benefits anticipated from the bombings. The dilemma faced by Israel following the kidnapping of approximately two hundred fifty hostages was similar, but not exactly the same as the dilemma faced by the Allies and other democracies in more conventional wars.

One major difference involves the media. During earlier conventional wars, captured prisoners were faceless and often nameless. Today's hostages have families that bring them to the attention of the world. These relatives understandably impose an enormous amount of pressure on their government to prioritize release of the hostages. No one can blame the families for such prioritization, but it makes it difficult for democracies to properly evaluate competing considerations.

In theory, there are several ways a democratic government could respond to the dilemma of defeating an enemy that holds hostages.

The most extreme approach, and one that has been advocated by some, is simply to ignore the hostages and fight the enemy without regard to their fate. Advocates of this view argue that if the hostages are ignored, future hostage taking will be disincentivized. But in a democracy, it is impossible to ignore hostage families.

A second related alternative is for the democracy to refuse to negotiate over the hostages, but to do everything in its power to rescue them, knowing full well that rescue attempts endanger their lives. This approach too is thought to disincentivize hostage taking.

A third alternative is to continue to attack the enemy, but to avoid targets near where hostages are thought to be held. This encourages the enemy to move the hostages near the most critical military targets.

A fourth approach is to negotiate for the hostages and be willing to exchange them for prisoners, while refusing to compromise strategic battlefield advantages. This is close to the approach taken by the Israeli government that led up to the Trump deal two years after October 7, 2023.

Finally, there is the approach advocated by many but not all hostage families. Namely, to prioritize the return of the hostages over military victory or advantage. Advocates of this approach argue that release of the hostages is more important than temporary military advantages, and that once the hostages are returned, the government can find justifications for continuing to battle the enemy. That too is close to the approach taken by Israel

There is no one perfect solution to this dilemma, especially in the imperfect world in which we live. If the international

community were united in opposing hostage taking and in support-
ing return of the hostages, perhaps that too would disincentivize
the illegal and immoral taking of hostages. But tragically, much of
the world—especially the media, academia, international organi-
zations, and the hard Left—seem more sympathetic to the hostage
takers than to the hostages. This sad reality makes the decisions of
democracies with regard to hostages even more difficult.

E. Israel Should Never Sacrifice Its Military Needs for Public Relations

Israel today is losing the war of public relations. In the court of
international opinion, and especially on many university campuses,
it is widely regarded as the absolutely worst nation in the world—
worse than Iran, China, Cuba, Rwanda, Russia, or Belarus. This
false ranking is not a function of any reality. It is a result of the
pervasive antisemitism that has plagued the world for two and a
half millennia and is now focused on Israel, which is the Jew among
nations. Even after October 7, and before Israel responded to the
worst massacre of Jews since the Holocaust, Israel was blamed for
the mass murder of its own citizens. To be sure, there was some
sympathy for the Jewish dead, but it was short-lived. Before very
long, the attacks on Israel continued in full force. Even early in the
war, Israel was falsely accused of genocide, deliberately targeting
women and children, starvation, and other evils that commonly
accompany military actions, particularly against terrorists who hide
among civilians. Even before the war, Israel's enemies characterized
the Gaza Strip as an "open-air prison," despite the absence of any
Israeli presence. Hamas was busy building terror tunnels, firing rockets at Jewish civilians, and planning the October 7 massacres and
kidnappings. Hamas was in complete control, yet Israel was blamed
for the plight of Gaza and the attacks of October 7.

Even those who believe Israel acted disproportionately must

acknowledge that the defamations against Israel have been even more disproportionate. Israel is, has always been, and will always be a subject of double-standard criticism and condemnation. The excuses and attempted justifications for this discrimination have been multifold: Israel gets US aid, Israel purports to be a democracy, Israel holds itself out as a paradigm of human rights, Israel is a western nation. But even if Israel were none of the above, the fact that it is the nation-state of the Jewish people would be enough to demand of it what is never demanded of other nations, namely perfection during the fog of a war fought against terrorists who hide behind civilians.

Israel will <u>never</u> win the war of public opinion. That does not mean that it should not demand to be assessed objectively, honestly, and reasonably by that biased court. But it will never succeed. And for that reason, it should never compromise one iota of its security in exchange for anticipated PR benefits. It should do what is right by its own extraordinarily high standards of morality and should expect no PR benefits for acting pursuant to these high standards.

Historically, Jewish communities around the world, including in Israel, have imposed upon themselves a standard of morality and self-sacrifice unparalleled by any other community or nation. It has gotten little in return. Indeed, quite the opposite. The enemies of Israel have benefitted from their own low standards. There are European nations that have and will continue to give the Palestinians the gift of recognizing a phantom Palestinian state, without demanding anything in return, even recognition of Israel as the nation-state of the Jewish people. In addition to numerous nations rewarding terrorism by recognition, every international organization has demonstrated bias against the Jewish state. This includes the United Nations, the International Criminal Court, the International Court of Justice, and numerous other governmental and non-governmental entities. No reasonable person can dispute the reality of this bigotry. Nor can Israel do much to counteract this sad state of affairs. The only thing Israel can do is to remain stronger than all of its combined enemies. It must not only be the Sparta of the Middle East, indeed of the world, but it must also be its Athens.

F. Israel Must Be Sparta and Athens

In Ancient Greece, Athens was known for its philosophers, scientists, and theorists of democracy. Sparta was known for its military prowess, its bravery, and its ability to defend itself against enemies. In today's world, in order to be Sparta, a nation must also be Athens. Wars are no longer merely battles of physical strength. They are conflicts in which intelligence, technology, and science prevail.

It is precisely because Israel is Athens—a world leader in science, technology, and democracy—that it is also Sparta. This has been shown dramatically by Israel's technological superiority over its enemies, as reflected by its targeted attacks on its enemy's leaders and terrorist murderers.

This was illustrated most dramatically by how it turned Hezbollah's military communication systems into weapons against the terrorists themselves. It was also demonstrated by its use of sophisticated intelligence to locate and neutralize leaders of Hamas and Hezbollah. Even the killing of Yahya Sinwar, though somewhat fortuitous, was facilitated by a small drone that flew into the house in which he was hiding. It doesn't always succeed, as illustrated by its failure to kill Hamas leaders in Qatar, but its success rate is extraordinary.

Israel is a tiny country, both in size and population, with few natural resources and with borders that are difficult to defend. Yet since even before its establishment in 1948, it depended on its academic as much as its military prowess to overcome these disadvantages by relying on education, innovation, and planning.

It hasn't always worked, as evidenced by its intelligence failures on October 7, 2023—failures that diminished its deterrence and encouraged adventurism by Iran and its proxies. Over the past year, though, the IDF's deterrence has been restored largely by its technological successes.

Everything would change, however, if Iran were ever allowed to develop and threaten to deploy a nuclear arsenal. There is no completely certain technological defense to nuclear-tipped ballistic missiles. If even one made it through Israel's excellent defense system—enhanced by America—it could mean the end of Israel.

As Iran's former president warned: "Israel is a one bomb state." Even one successful nuclear attack on Tel Aviv or Jerusalem would constitute an existential catastrophe for Israel.

Nor can Israel hope to deter such an attack by threatening to retaliate against Tehran with a nuclear attack on that population center. As Prime Minister Begin said in 1981, after he ordered the preventive destruction of the Iraqi nuclear reactor at Osirak, "Israel will never incinerate millions of innocent children." Being Athens—with its deep commitment to democracy, values, and humanity—has its drawbacks when it comes to deterrence.

There are limits to what a democracy will do—limits that tyrannies do not have—even in response to attacks on its citizens. That is why, Begin said, Israel must prevent rather than respond to a nuclear attack, as it did in Iraq and Syria, and as it must do with Iran.

Israel, along with America, is currently using both military attacks and technology in a continuing effort to thwart Iran's nuclear ambitions. Cyber-attacks and targeted assassinations were not enough. A military attack on Iran's nuclear facilities was required. Such an attack made use of Israel's technological and scientific advantages, but in the end its success depended as much on the courage of its pilots and other soldiers. We do not know for certain precisely how much of Israel's nuclear capacity has been destroyed by the combined military attacks by the United States and Israel. But we do know that it has been set back.

It is the creative combination of Athens and Sparta—technology and bravery—that has allowed Israel to implement the blessing of the Psalmist: "God will give the Jewish people strength." Only then will they be "blessed with peace." Jewish history throughout the ages and Israeli history of the last century have proved beyond any doubt that morality alone will not prevent antisemites and anti-Zionists from trying to destroy us. We need physical strength to back up our morality.

We had morality on our side during the Holocaust, and we had morality on our side on October 7. The reason we will never again experience a holocaust is not because our morality has improved. It is because the Israeli army is stronger than its enemies and the Jewish people around the world use their strength in the interest of self-preservation.

Zionism, Judaism, and the Jewish people are under attack all over the world, especially from the Left and most especially from young people who represent the increasing dangers we face in the future. The response requires a continuing combination of Athens and Sparta. Israel and the Jewish people must continue to excel at science, technology, education, morality, and democracy.

Israel cannot afford—at least not yet—to turn their swords into plowshares or their nuclear weapons into nuclear medicine. It must use its Athenian attributes to make Israel an even stronger Sparta.

My interpretation of King David's Psalm is influenced by history. The Jewish nation will only have peace if they are strong. Jewish weakness has always been an invitation to disaster. As Prime Minister Benjamin Netanyahu always reminds us: if Hamas would put down its arms, there would be peace. But if Israel were to put down its arms, there would be genocide. We have seen the latter come true over and over again. Jews without the ability to defend themselves have been constant victims over the millennia. The book of Esther describes how Jews rose up against their intended genocidal murderers and killed them first. The Talmud demands that if a person rises to kill you, you should rise and kill him first. This is preemption and prevention, subjects I have been writing about for more than sixty years.

Prevention and preemption lie at the core not only of Israel's need to protect itself, but also at the core for the need of Jewish communities around the world to protect themselves from the increasing enmity and antisemitism of so many people in so many places.

The Jewish people and their state should never ask permission to take necessary preventive actions. If they err and overreact, they can apologize after the fact. That is what other nations have done throughout history and that is what Jews must do now and in the future.

There are more than enough museums and memorials to Jews who have been the victims of inaction. Let the enemies of the Jewish nation build their museums and memorials, while victorious Jews succeed in preventing recurrences of past pogroms and genocides. It is better to be wrongly condemned by bigots than to be memorialized by them with crocodile tears.

G. An Overview of the Dynamics

There are pincer movements against Jews and their nation-state from both the Right and Left. The right-wing component is led by influential bigots such as Tucker Carlson, Candace Owens, and Kanye West. The left-wing component is led by so-called Democratic socialists such as Zohran Mamdani, the Squad, and Islamicists including Ilhan Omar. They have little in common other than their hatred for Jews, Israel, and American support for the nation-state of the Jewish people. Together, they constitute a formidable pincer movement reminiscent of the extremism that led to the Holocaust and the Stalin purges of Jews. The center is weakening, as this generation of young people do and as many others have tradition-ally done: eschew moderation and reason in favor of extremism and emotion. The end result is generally violent scapegoating of the kind we are already seeing on many university campuses, and on the streets of some cities. It poses a real danger not only to Jews, but to democracy, liberty, and the rule of law, because Jews have not only been history's traditional scapegoat; they have also been its canary in the mine. The mine is quickly filling with lethal gases. We must take action to prevent explosions and suffocations of the kind the world experienced nearly a century ago. "Never again" will turn into "again and again" unless we take preventive action now. Right now! Before it is too late. Underreaction, silence (*"sha -shtill"*), and protecting the status of community leaders were enemies back in the 1930s. They remain enemies today, though in different forms. Today, it is the failure to recognize and combat extremism by those on both sides of the political spectrum that poses the greatest danger.

Classic conservatism, as personified by Willam Buckley, and classic liberalism, as personified by the Kennedy brothers and Bill Clinton, have historically eschewed extremism, and provided guardrails against antisemitism. These guardrails have now been weakened, and the barbarians are at the gates. Mainstream conser-vatives and liberals are fighting back, but they are losing where it counts most for the future—among the young. That is the way it was in much of Europe in the early 1930s. Not so much in the United States, where a classic liberal, FDR, defeated a classic conservative, Herbert Hoover, in 1932, as the depression spread throughout the world. Economic turmoil, such as that which followed the First World War, feeds extremism. We are not in a depression now, but if economic turmoil were to befall the world, it is unlikely that a current moderate leader could save us from the blight of extremism, as FDR did in the 1930s. We are ripe for the rise of the hard Right or Left, as Europeans were back then.

This dangerous reality poses an existential dilemma for all classic conservatives and liberals, but most particularly, for Jews who are the first victims of extremism, and especially for liberal Jews who have long considered the center-left to be their comfortable home. Most Jews have been moderate Democrats who support much of the traditional Democratic platform over the Republican one. But they support Israel, oppose racial quotas, favor meritocracy, and seek protection from the police. They worry that if the Democrats return to power, they will be led by the likes of Zohran Mamdani, AOC, the Squad, Elizabeth Warren, and Bernie Sanders. But if the Republicans retain power, they will cut health care, impose unfair immigration policies, establish religion, curtail gay and transgender rights, limit abortion, and take other actions with which they disagree. They feel as politically homeless as many Jews felt in Europe in the 1930s—isolated between the Brown of fascism and the Red of communism. When the Jews of Italy faced that dilemma in the 1920s, some voted for Mussolini, much to their later regret, as many Jews later regretted their support for Lenin and Stalin in the 1920s.

Many young "progressive" Jews voted for NYC Mayoral candidate Zohran Mamdani, despite his long record of anti-Israel activities and his refusal to condemn anti-Jewish rhetoric. Non-Jewish New Yorkers also voted for him, <u>despite</u>, not <u>because</u> of, his bigoted anti-Jewish history. Similarly, in the 1932 German election, many "decent" Germans voted for the Nazi Party, not because, but despite, its antisemitic platform. They favored <u>other</u> aspects of the Nazi program such as full employment and a strong military. They did not prioritize the antisemitic hatred, much like many Mamdani voters refused to prioritize his hatred. They too may come to regret their votes.

Many New Yorkers are afraid that Mamdani will fail and destroy this beloved city. I am more afraid that he may <u>succeed</u> and improve the city in some ways, as Hitler apparently succeeded, at least to some degree, in improving the German economy during his first years as chancellor. This success strengthened him and incentivized more Germans to accept and act on his Jew-hatred. I fear a similar phenomenon with regard to Mamdani's anti-Zionism.

Many centrist liberals and conservatives, especially Jews, do not know for whom they should vote as the least worst or least dangerous option. They don't want to stay home. They would like to try to influence their party to move toward the middle, but they are frustrated by what appears to be an unstoppable trend toward both extremes.

Many liberal Jews are facing the dilemma of which party to support, or more realistically, to oppose in the 2026 congressional elections. If the Democrats win the House, some very bad people—including virulent antisemites—will be elevated to influential positions, including committee chairmanships. But if the Republicans maintain control over the House, they will enact legislation with which many of us disagree. At the moment, I think the former is more dangerous—at least to my values and priorities—than the latter. I also think that another democratic defeat might help move that party more to the center. No one can be sure of these ever-shifting dynamics, but we must cast votes and lend support based on imperfect information and uncertain prediction, just as the Jews of Europe had to do in the 1920s and 1930s. But unlike the Jews back then, we have somewhat more influence—limited as it may be—on events than they did. We have already used that limited influence on some universities and other institutions in an effort to combat rising campus antisemitism. Whether we can strengthen and broaden that influence remain to be seen.

It is part of the purpose of this short book to consider constructive steps that can be taken to offset the insidious influences of both the extreme Right and Left. This also part of its purpose—to paraphrase Maimonides—to help serve as a guide to the perplexed, as many decent people have become in this age of divisive extremism in which it is demanded that everyone take sides. If you chose the "wrong" side, you are cancelled, dismissed, and condemned, especially by the Left.

Many of us grew up in simpler times when choices were obvious. There was good and evil. Nazism, Stalinism, McCarthyism, antisemitism, and racism were evil. Liberalism was good. Conservatism was acceptable, though no one I knew actually voted for conservative or Republican candidates (with a few exceptions). But we respected Eisenhower, Taft, Dole and both Bushes—and even grudgingly Goldwater.

There was little nuance, complexity or ambiguity, even on Israel: Democrats supported Israel; so did most Republicans, but not as strongly as Democrats. Voting was easy. We were knee-jerk Democrats, though many of us voted for liberal and pro-Israel Republicans like Jacob Javits and Nelson Rockefeller. No cognitive dissonance or heart-wrenching decisions. No "on the one hand, on the other." Life was simpler and so was politics for liberals, especially Jews. Not anymore. Today, it is largely a question of priorities. There are no perfect candidates or parties. Each has their virtues and vices. It depends on which virtues are most important and which vices are most frightening. There is little agreement on these questions of degree. Some could never vote for a particular party or candidate. Most can vote for what they regard as the lesser of evils. A few can't bring themselves to vote at all. Almost no one I know is completely comfortable with the current options.

H: Call to Arms and to a New Proactive Morality to Prevent a Recurrence of the Tragic Past

In this book, and others I have written, I explore the sources of contemporary Jew-hatred, Israel demonization, and other threats to Jewish communities around the world. I demonstrate why I believe things are likely to get worse, as they did in Germany during the late 1930s. I do not believe they will culminate in another genocidal holocaust, but I do believe that when these young bigots grow into influential adults, they will increase the hatred against Jews and their nation-state.

I also try to provide what I believe are appropriate responses to this growing threat. There is no perfect solution just as there was none in the 1930s. But we can do more and better than they did because we have learned the dangerous lessons of history and must be determined not to repeat them. Silence and acquiescence are not options in the face of these growing threats. Nor is simply responding to attacks. We must take both responsive and proactive steps to avoid any risk that the disastrous past will be repeated, even in part.

American Jews and supporters of Israel are currently secure, influential, and self-satisfied. So were the Jews in Germany in 1933. That's why so many of them stayed on, at least until Kristallnacht persuaded them that remaining in Germany was not a feasible option. By then it was too late for many. Some managed to escape. Most of those who stayed were murdered in the years to come.

We are currently near the beginning, rather than near the end, of what is a considerable threat to the future of Jews and their nation-state. Although we cannot predict with absolute accuracy the long, middle, or even short-term consequences of this threat, we must take it extremely seriously in order to minimize the resulting damage. This book offers a road map, based both on history and current reality, for addressing these issues now!

I don't know whether I can have any real influence on the Jewish future, but I will surely use every resource I have to try to have a positive influence going forward. Hence, this book and others I plan to write along with activities I plan to pursue in the years left to me. I will not be frightened into inaction. Neither should you.

Like all my books about current events, this is a work in progress. Realities on the ground, in the air, in cyberspace, in the media and at the polls are ever-changing and in large part unpredictable. I always try to adapt my writing to these dynamics, while adhering to my fundamental principles and beliefs.

To adapt my principles and beliefs to the current reality requires an acknowledgment that the Jewish community and its state are not playing on a fair and level playing field. Much of the world has turned against us, immorally, unfairly, prejudicially, and with closed minds. Justice will not prevail if we play by rules that are relevant only on a non-existent level playing field. We must adapt our morality to the new reality of anti-Israel, anti-Jewish, and anti-fairness immorality.

How to make these necessary changes without compromising our just standards of morality and principle is the difficult question. We must face it squarely and realistically. We tried to maintain our morality in the face of unmitigated immorality in the 1930s and 1940s. Mahatma Gandhi believed and wrote that "Jews should have offered themselves to the butcher's knife" of Naziism. That would have shown the world that Jews were on the right side of morality. Gandhi was himself something of a bigot, who did not like Jews or Blacks and strongly opposed the creation of Israel, even after the Holocaust. He was also a hypocrite who had no right to tell Jews what they should do morally in the face of what he later acknowledged was the "greatest crime of our time." Gandhi's naïve foolishness illustrates the futility of maintaining a single high, if not impossible, standard of morality in the face of the greatest of immoralities.

When I taught a freshman seminar at Harvard College entitled, "Where does your morality come from?" I would confront the students with the following hypothetical (based on a question posed by

Ivan to Alyosha in Dostoyevsky's *Brothers Karamazov*)[1]: You are the leader of the Jewish underground in 1943 Berlin while Jews were being gassed in Auschwitz and Treblinka. Your intelligence sources tell you that the only way to stop the genocide is to start blowing up German kindergartens and killing innocent German children. You believe that this immoral tactic would work, because Nazis love their children. Would you try it?

The challenge of today's immoral world is to adapt our morality so as to enable us to respond to today's immorality without unduly compromising our own principles. It is a difficult challenge, but one that must be accepted if we are to survive. We cannot afford to repeat the past, and so we must learn its lessons. The most prominent among them is never to respond to a nuclear attack, even a nuclear moral attack, with a kitchen knife. We must be stronger than our enemies, both morally and physically. If we are defeated physically, as we were by the Holocaust, our higher morality will accomplish nothing. We must prevent defeat by all means possible, even if that requires us to adapt our morality in order to defeat their immorality.

Another current example of adapting old moralities to immoral

---

1 Dostoyevsky's original question was: "I challenge you—answer me: imagine that you are charged with building the edifice of human destiny, whose ultimate aim is to bring people happiness, to give them peace and contentment at last, but that in order to achieve this it is essential and unavoidable to torture just one little speck of creation, that same little child beating her breast with her little fists, and imagine that this edifice has to be erected on her unexpurgated tears. Would you agree to be the architect under those conditions? Tell me honestly!" Alyosha, like Kant, says "no." Ivan, like Bentham, implies "yes." A more relevant contemporary question is: Would you risk killing twenty-five innocent Palestinian children in order to rescue ten innocent Israeli hostages who were being held beneath a Gaza kindergarten?

new tactics was the decision by Israel to target Hamas leaders who were being given asylum in Qatar. Much of the world condemned this attack on a civilian neighborhood of a sovereign ally of the US, but it was morally justified. The targeted Hamas leaders included mass murderers who helped organize the barbarisms of October 7, and who pledged to organize more October 7s in the future. The IDF took extraordinary measures to minimize civilian casualties— measures that included the use of small ammunitions that may have helped some of the leaders to escape.

Had Hitler and other leading Nazis been given sanctuary by Switzerland, while the German army was still killing Americans and Brits, its allies would have applauded the targeting of these Nazis in downtown Zurich. Morality, to be an effective check on military action, must be adapted to the realities of enemy and morality, while preserving the essential components of justice. President Barack Obama ordered the assassination (not the capture) of Osama bin Laden, who posed no current threat. He was hiding in Pakistan. If that attack in a sovereign nation was justified, then surely a targeted assassination attempt in a nation that was deliberately harboring ongoing terrorist leaders was more justified. The difference is that it failed to kill the Hamas leaders, though it may have incentivized Qatar to put more pressure on Hamas to make a deal.

The real world cannot live by Kant's categorical imperative or Gandhi's suicidal preachments. Jews, especially because so much of our blood has been spilled so cheaply and so inconsequentially, must live by the only morality that will prevent a recurrence: "if someone comes to kill you, rise up and kill them first."

Chapter 1

Open Letter to President Trump Prior to His Decision to Bomb Iranian Nuclear Facilities

Dear Mr. President,

You are about to make a decision for which you will be remembered by history. Your legacy will either be as a world leader who saved, or failed to save, many lives. The decision concerns Iran's intention to develop a nuclear arsenal. There can be no reasonable doubt that Iran's mullahs are determined to obtain nuclear weapons, despite their assurances to the contrary. Nor can Israel, which is the intended target of an Iranian bomb, be expected to rely on deterrence or containment. Iran must be prevented from achieving their dangerous goal.

Obviously, it would be better if the mullahs could be stopped by negotiation rather than military action. Previous negotiations resulted in a terrible deal under President Barack Obama. You yourself understood that under the Obama deal, Iran would almost certainly have obtained a nuclear arsenal, and so you quite correctly withdrew from the agreement. Now there are rumors that your administration is working on a "better" deal—longer and stronger. But unless your deal includes the complete and total destruction of all Iranian nuclear facilities, there will be no guarantee that its scientists could not surreptitiously use civilian nuclear infrastructure to build military weaponry. The only deal that would prevent this catastrophe would be one modeled on the agreement made with Libya back in 2003. That deal completely dismantled Libya's nuclear facilities and made it impossible for them to weaponize nuclear energy infrastructure. Anything short of that will create an unacceptable risk.

We urge you to use your incredible negotiating skills to achieve the goal that you have set out: namely, a 100 percent certainty that Iran will never get a nuclear bomb. You should give the mullahs a short period of time to dismantle and destroy, subject to American inspection, their entire nuclear program. If they refuse or fail to do so, the military option should be deployed.

Nearly a century ago, the British and French governments faced a similar decision with Germany, and they failed, costing tens of millions of lives.

A military attack on Germany in the mid-1930s, when its war machine was still weak, might have saved many of these lives. Here is what Reich Minister of Propaganda Joseph Goebbels wrote in his memoir:

> In 1933 a French premier ought to have said (and if I had been the French premier, I would have said it): "The new Reich chancellor is the man who wrote *Mein Kampf*, which says this and that. This man cannot be tolerated in our vicinity. Either he disappears or we March!" But they didn't do it. They left us alone and let us slip through the risky zone, and we were able to sail around all dangerous

reefs. And when we were done, and well armed, better than they, then they started the war!

The rest is tragic history. Germany built up its armed forces without countermeasures by its intended enemies, conquered most of Western Europe, and killed millions of people. Most of those deaths could certainly have been avoided had Great Britain and France engaged in preventive military action before Germany became "well armed" and capable of inflicting so much damage on the world.

At the moment in history when Great Britain and France could have prevented the horrendous harm done by Nazi Germany, there was no way of knowing in advance the extent of what Adolf Hitler would do.

Yes, Hitler wrote *Mein Kampf*, but many would-be conquerors do not follow through on their threats. (Recall the threat of the Soviet Union's Premier Nikita Khrushchev to "bury" the United States, yet he backed away from a nuclear confrontation over Cuba.)

There was no way of predicting, with any degree of certainty, that Hitler would turn his belligerent rhetoric into military invasions of Poland, Europe, and then the Soviet Union—and ultimately the Holocaust. It was, as it always is, a question of cost-benefit probabilities. This was a classic case of a false negative: implicitly predicting that Hitler would not do what, in fact, he did, and failing to take action in an effort to prevent it. If France and Great Britain had accurately predicted Hitler's actual harm correctly, they would almost certainly have taken preventive military action even if the cost were high—because it would never have been nearly as high as it turned out to be in the absence of such action.

But history is blind to the predictive future. Had Great Britain and France engaged in preventive military action in the 1930s that resulted in the deaths of, say, fifteen thousand British and French soldiers and civilians, the leaders who undertook such a military campaign would have been condemned as warmongers, because no one would ever know how many deaths they prevented by the sacrifice of those fifteen thousand lives. Ignorance of the hypothetical future is often the reason for failure to act in the present. That is the dilemma of failing to take preventive military action.

Mr. President, we are once again at a decisive decision point. And you are the decider. We urge you to do the right thing: take the necessary actions that will assure, with absolute certainty, that Iran will never obtain a nuclear arsenal, even if the only way to secure that certainly ends up being through military action.

Chapter 2

Israel's Preemptive Attack on Iran Justified

In my just-published book, *The Preventive State*, I make the following case for a preemptive military strike against Iran's nascent nuclear arsenal:

> If [diplomacy] fails and if it becomes likely that Iran is about to cross the threshold into making a deliverable nuclear weapon, the pressure on Israel to act, with or without the assistance and/or approval of the United States, will increase considerably . . .
>
> No democracy can afford to wait until such a threat against its civilian population is imminent. Both Israel and the United States should have the right under international law to protect their civilians and soldier from a threatened nuclear holocaust, and that right must include—if that is the only realistic option—preemptive military action of the sort taken by Israel against the Iraqi nuclear reactor at Osirak in 1981, especially if such action

can again be taken without an unreasonable number of civilian casualties.

International law authorizes preemptive military action when reasonably necessary to prevent nuclear attacks on civilian populations. Even if the number of likely casualties on both sides is high in the current war between Israel and Iran, there may be a cost-benefit case for preventive military action, because the cost of not taking such action may be far greater.

In some respects, Israel's recent attack can be justified as reactive rather than preemptive or preventive. It was a legitimate response to Iran's direct missile attacks during this past year, as well as its indirect attacks through its surrogates in Yemen, Lebanon, and Gaza. In any event, preemptive action was necessary.

A prime example of the cost of the false negative of not taking preventive military action is provided by not-so-distant history. In the mid-1930s, following Adolf Hitler's rise to power, he began building a military machine in violation of the Versailles Treaty.

Britain and France were strong militarily but war weary. They could have taken preventive military action against a still weak, but war-hungry, Germany. Joseph Goebbels, Hitler's chief propagandist, was surprised "they didn't do it"—until it was too late. Tens of millions of innocent people died as a result of this "false negative" failure to act.

Had Israel failed to act against Iran, such a "false negative" could have resulted in millions of deaths from a nuclear armed fanatical regime that has pledged to destroy "the Zionist devil." We'll never know for certain what harms Israel's preemptive action may have prevented, because history is blind to the predictive future.

Had Great Britain and France decided to take preventive military action in the mid-1930s, and done so successfully, no one would ever know what was prevented. If a leader, say Britain's Winston

Churchill, had been able to act on his fear that Hitler would kill tens of millions of people unless he was stopped at that time by preventive military action, the leader would have been disbelieved, even mocked, as George W. Bush was for taking military action against Iraq's suspected nuclear arsenal in 2003.

Had Great Britain and France engaged in preventive military action in the 1930s that resulted in, say, the deaths of ten thousand German and five thousand British and French soldiers and civilians, the leaders who undertook such a military adventure would been condemned as warmongers, because no one would ever know how many deaths they prevented by the sacrifice of those fifteen thousand lives.

That is the dilemma of invisible false negatives in failing to take preventive military action. A preventive attack would not have been cost free, and it was not undertaken, because the British and French did not accurately predict and assess the cost of not acting. The result was a catastrophic false negative.

Benjamin Netanyahu has been faulted—largely by left-wing Democrats and radicals—on the grounds that he acted too quickly, failing to wait for the outcome of talks which might have resulted in a diplomatic resolution. But a satisfactory deal that would have absolutely assured that Iran would never obtain nuclear weapons was never likely, because Iran insisted on its "right" to enrich—and enrichment is a path to weaponization.

It seems clear that Iran was using the negotiations to buy time to move toward a nuclear arsenal. Its goal was to get close enough to weaponization so as to make it too risky to attack its radioactive facilities. So, Netanyahu was right, as a matter of law, morality, and diplomacy, to do what he did, when he did it. And so was the United States in targeting three nuclear sites.

Chapter 3

What Hypocritical AOC Is Shamelessly Ignoring When She Calls Trump's Iran Strikes "Unconstitutional"

Even as a tenuous cease-fire between Iran and Israel appears to hold, Democrats in the US Congress are falling over themselves to condemn President Donald Trump for the strikes that made this chance at peace possible.

Trump's Iran attack is "unauthorized and unconstitutional," said the No. 2 Democrat in the House, Katherine Clark.

"Donald Trump's decision to launch direct military action against Iran without congressional approval is a clear violation of the Constitution," added Jim Himes, the ranking Democrat on the Intelligence Committee.

Congresswoman Alexandria Ocasio-Cortez went further, claiming Trump's action "is absolutely and clearly grounds for impeachment."

That's absurd. The framers of the Constitution understood the difference between Congress officially declaring war and the commander-in-chief of the armed forces taking military action in defense of our nation. The original draft of Article 1 allocated to Congress the power to "make war." But James Madison, the father of our Constitution, demanded that it be amended to "declar[ing] war" so that the president would have broader authority to take actions in defense of our country.

During the subsequent two and a quarter centuries, various presidents and members of Congress have interpreted this division of authority differently, and many presidents have taken military action without declarations of war or even congressional authorization. In recent years, Democratic presidents Bill Clinton and Barack Obama authorized significant military actions without any complaints by Democratic members of Congress, including several who have now whined about Trump having acted unconstitutionally.

This is hypocrisy on stilts and reflects the extreme partisan weaponization of the Constitution, even over foreign and military policies. What President Trump did is not different in kind or degree from what previous presidents—both Democrats and Republicans—have done without congressional authorization. The last time Congress declared war was shortly after Japan bombed Pearl Harbor. There were no declarations of war over Korea, Vietnam, Iraq, Afghanistan, Granada or Panama. In fact, it is unlikely we will ever again see another declaration of war.

Perhaps Congress will now do what it has done since the end of World War II: pass resolutions authorizing limited military action by the president. Though, these hybrid resolutions are not authorized by the Constitution either, and it is unlikely that they carry much legal weight.

Indeed, all this handwringing on the Left will come to nothing. The courts, especially the Supreme Court, are reluctant to interfere with executive decisions involving military actions, even those that involve boots on the ground for considerable periods of time. So, by all means, let's continue to debate the wisdom of Trump's decision as a matter of policy, but let's not improperly weaponize a constitutional provision that was never intended to prevent presidents from taking actions deemed necessary to defend our nation, such as the surgical, one-off bombing of three Iranian nuclear facilities.

As a matter of policy, a president should not be required to show his hand before ordering a surprise military attack of this kind. The consequences, both short and long term, of President Trump's bold decision remain to be seen, but he surely had the power to make that decision if he deemed it in the best interests of the country.

Congress can now hold hearings, both open and closed, to assess the president's actions, but only hypocritical Democrats, and hard-Left radicals afflicted with Trump Derangement Syndrome will argue that what Trump did was unconstitutional or unlawful. It was not.

Chapter 4

Recognition of Palestinian State Threatens Hostages, Rewards Terrorism

France, England, Canada, Australia, and other American allies have recently "recognized" a nonexistent Palestinian "state." The immediate consequence was to incentivize Hamas to reject US peace deals and to endanger many lives.

As Marco Rubio put it: "Talks with Hamas fell apart on the day Macron made the unilateral decision that he's going to recognize the Palestinian state. . . . So those messages, while largely symbolic in their minds, actually have made it harder to get peace and harder to achieve a deal with Hamas."

I was in Israel to meet with Israeli leaders and to try to visit Gaza when this occurred. After several meetings, I was confirmed in my strong belief that the decision by these countries to recognize "Palestine" emboldened Hamas to persist in its prior refusal to release the hostages in exchange for a ceasefire.

Both US President Donald Trump and his envoy Steve Witkoff

have placed the blame squarely at the feet of Hamas for rejecting US proposals to end the current impasse.

Polls show that Palestinians, both in Gaza and the West Bank, would vote overwhelmingly to be governed by Hamas rather than the Palestinian Authority if free elections were held. This would be even more certain if Hamas is credited with securing a state—something the PA could not accomplish over the many years it has been in power.

Even if Hamas itself cares more about destroying Israel than having a Palestinian state recognized, they would gain much from having secured recognition.

Recognition of statehood was widely and correctly seen as rewarding Hamas for its massacres of October 7. It sent a loud message to terrorist groups around the world that terrorism is more effective than negotiation.

It will encourage more October 7s—as Hamas has already promised—not only against Israel, but against other nations that are threatened by terrorists with grievances, which includes most democracies.

Recognizing a Palestinian state without even conditioning such recognition on the release of the hostages or in the Palestinians recognizing Israel will ensure continuing belligerence in Gaza. Hamas doesn't care how many Gazans are killed.

To the contrary, they believe their cause benefits from the death of martyrs. That is why they use civilians as human shields and prohibit them from seeking shelter in the tunnels that protect their terrorists from Israeli bombings.

When these immoral tactics—prohibited by the laws of war—are rewarded and incentivized by giving Hamas what it wants—credit for achieving statehood without giving up anything—it gives Hamas a major quid without quo.

No wonder Trump, the master of quid pro quo deal-making,

is opposed to giving the Palestinians something for nothing. This is especially troubling, since the Palestinian leadership has turned down offers of statehood in return for real peace on numerous occasions.

As former president Bill Clinton recently put it:

> The only time Yasser Arafat didn't tell me the truth was when he promised he was going to accept the peace deal that we had worked out. Which would have given the Palestinians a state in 96 percent of the West Bank and 4 percent of Israel. . . . So they would have the effect of the same land of all the West Bank. They would have a capital in East Jerusalem . . . all this was offered including . . . a capital in East Jerusalem and two of the four quadrants of the old city of Jerusalem confirmed by the Israeli prime minister Ehud Barak and his cabinet, and they said no, and I think part of it is that Hamas did not care about a homeland for the Palestinians. They wanted to kill Israelis and make Israel uninhabitable.

What benefits—other than virtue signaling to their left-wing and Muslim domestic constituents—do these countries expect to achieve by the hollow act of recognition? It will only make it harder for positions on both sides.

The Palestinians will be encouraged to persist in the terrorist tactics that produced recognition, and the Israeli right wing will demand annexation of the disputed territories that would comprise the theoretically recognized "state"—a "state" without recognized borders and without a recognized governing authority.

It is a recipe for anarchy, terrorism, and Islamic extremism with no counterbalancing benefits. It makes a two-state solution more difficult to achieve because a Hamas-controlled state would never recognize Israel as the nation-state of the Jewish people, and Israel would never recognize a "state" that was created—invented—without direct negotiations and reciprocal commitments. So the virtue signaling and electoral pandering of these hypocritical governments will surely backfire and cause more deaths and suffering on both sides.

It is fitting that these phony recognitions were announced from the podium of the UN General Assembly—the same forum that declared Zionism to be form of racism, that welcomed a Palestinian terrorist leader wielding a gun, that platformed Holocaust-denying Iranians, and that has served as the modern-day version of the notoriously anti-Semitic Der Stërmer of Nazi Germany. Following the decision to equate Zionism with racism, the Israeli representative to the UN ascended the podium and tore up the text of the resolution. Several years later, it was rescinded.

The false equation did little harm aside from damaging the credibility of the UN. It won't be as easy to rescind the dangerous recognitions that will tarnish the UN—and will risk the lives of Israelis and Palestinians. Shame on France, Great Britain, Canada, Australia, and other countries that will have the blood of innocent people on their hands.

Chapter 5

"When the Judges Ruled, There Was Famine"

The Book of Ruth begins with an ominous warning: "In the days when the judges ruled, there was famine in the land."

History shows that judges make poor leaders. Thomas Jefferson understood this when he tried to limit the influence of the "midnight judges" appointed by John Adams. Andrew Jackson refused to implement a Supreme Court decision that he believed undercut his policy toward Native American tribes. Abraham Lincoln responded to what he regarded as the overreaching of judges by suspending the writ of habeas corpus. Franklin Roosevelt threatened to pack the Supreme Court when the justices tried to dismantle his congressionally enacted New Deal.

Now, many district court judges are determined to thwart the policies of President Donald Trump. Judicial efforts to thwart executive and legislative actions have occurred frequently in our history, as have executive and legislative responses to such judicial activism.

Under Article 3 of the United States Constitution, judges are supposed to play a critical role in checking and balancing the excesses of the other branches. Their central responsibility is to enforce the procedural safeguards of the Bill of Rights, most particularly those assuring due process, equal protection, and the right of dissent. They have no legitimate business interfering with the substantive policies of the executive or legislative branches.

There was a time in our history when the Supreme Court interpreted the Constitution to include what was known as substantive due process—a vague concept that presumed to empower judges to strike down legislation and executive action that they deemed "unreasonable" or otherwise violative of broad constitutional limitations, such as the sanctity of property and contracts. Under these interpretations, they held unconstitutional many liberal and progressive reforms such as child labor restrictions and other protections of workers and consumers.

Liberals were furious at this expansion of judicial authority, and many Democrats demanded that restrictions be placed on judicial activism and overreach. During Franklin Roosevelt's presidency, dissenting justices, led by Louis Brandeis, the Supreme Court's most liberal member, called for judicial restraint and opposed what they regarded as the misapplication of substantive due process to the policies and actions of elected officials. The Brandeis view prevailed, but only after Roosevelt threatened to pack the court with additional justices who would sustain his policies. The result was a change in the voting patterns of several justices—which historians labeled "the switch in time that saved nine."

Now the shoe seems to be on the other foot. It is left-wing judges who are seeking to thwart the right-wing policies and actions of a Republican president. They do not explicitly invoke substantive due process—they wouldn't dare in light of the well-known history. But their actions smack of that rejected concept. They disapprove of Trump's deportation, defunding, firing, and other executive actions that they regard as un-American and unfair—just as the conservative judges regarded Roosevelt's attack on the right of contract as un-American.

In both situations, judges, hostile to the substantive polices of the administration, searched for procedural and other reasons to halt or slow down the implementation of these "bad" policies. In the current situation, the Trump administration has sometimes provided the courts with justifications for their actions, by applying due process safeguards narrowly, or questionably. But every honest legal realist will have to acknowledge that many of these judicial decisions have been influenced by policy considerations. Judges look harder to find procedural objections to policies and actions of which they disapprove.

The bottom line is that neither party passes the shoe on the other foot test. Both praise judicial activism when it helps their side and rail against it when it hurts them. The Trump administration praised SCOTUS for ruling that Harvard's race-based affirmative action admissions program was unconstitutional, but it objected when the courts stayed the administration's cutting of funding to Harvard and other institutions. The Democrats cheered when the justices decided *Roe v. Wade* on questionable constitutional grounds, but they jeered when a later court ruled that there was no constitutional right to abortion. These changing attitudes are not about different general principles regarding judicial activism or restraint. They are about specific outcomes of highly politicized cases and controversies.

In the end, Brandeis had the correct approach: judicial restraint, regardless of the partisan or ideological consequences. He consistently voted to uphold laws and practices with which he had strong substantive disagreements, so long as they did not clearly violate express provisions of the Constitution. That is the proper role of unelected judges in a democracy.

The people—not the judges—should rule the land.

Chapter 6

My Battle to Buy Pierogi Might End Up in Court. Can a Martha's Vineyard Food Vendor Refuse to Sell to Me Because I'm a Zionist?

I have been going to the farmers market in Martha's Vineyard for nearly half a century. I buy corn, tomatoes, and homemade products. Until last week, every vendor at the market treated me with respect and loved to have my business. I spent about $100,000 on farm and home products over the years, so I was shocked when one vendor refused to sell me their pierogi.

It turns out that this particular vendor, Krem Miskevich, doesn't approve of Zionism—that is, support for Israel's right to exist as the nation-state of the Jewish people. To be a Zionist does not require agreement with Israel's policies or actions—just its right to be. I strongly believe in Zionism. It is an essential aspect of my religion. Jewish prayer, going back thousands of years, asks God to help the Jewish people return to Zion, which is Israel. The Jewish Bible and prayer book is filled with references to God's decision to give the Holy Land to the Jewish people. Indeed, the Bible warns that those who curse Israel shall be cursed. Israel is at least as central to Judaism as the Vatican is to Catholicism, as Mecca is to Islam, and as Salt Lake City is to Mormonism.

Jerusalem is mentioned in Jewish religious sources thousands of times. (Not in the Quran.) The very flag of Israel is based on the Jewish prayer shawl, the tallit. Its most basic symbols—the star of David and the menorah—are deeply religious in nature. To deny the religious connection between Zionism and Judaism is itself an act of antisemitism, as well as ignorance. So it is difficult to separate the religious, nationalistic, and political aspects of Zionism and Judaism. Not all Jews are Zionists, but not all Jews keep kosher or obey the Sabbath. That doesn't mean that keeping kosher isn't an important aspect of Judaism. So is Zionism. If a vendor refused to sell to all people who keep kosher, that would be unlawful, even though many Jews don't.

Accordingly, when Krem Miskevich refused to sell his pierogi to Zionists, they were engaged to a significant degree in religious discrimination, since most Jews are Zionists. To date, I'm aware of no court that has ruled on whether Zionists, who base their Zionism on the Jewish religion, are a protected class under the Constitution. That issue may be tested in court based on the vendor's refusal to serve me. If they had refused to serve a customer because he was Black or gay or Israeli or a Jew, that would be expressly prohibited by Massachusetts law, as well as the law in many other states.

This case is different from the supreme court case involving the baker who refused to design a cake for the marriage of a gay couple. Designing the cake involved artistic input and was therefore protected by the First Amendment. Selling already made pierogi that was sitting on the counter, is not protected speech. It is like refusing to rent to somebody based on race, religion, and other invidious factors. It is also wrong as a matter of morality: Vendors who hold themselves out as selling to the public should not discriminate on the basis of political or religious views. If they were to do so, there would have to be two pierogi stands at the farmers market—one that sells to non-Zionists only, and one that sells to Zionists as well.

After Miskevich's refusal to sell me their pierogi was made public, a number of people called to advise me that Miskevich has engaged in both anti-Semitic and anti-Zionist protests. They are among the leaders of an organization on the Vineyard that not only supports Hamas, but also protests Jewish cultural events that emphasize Jewish music, food, art, and other aspects of Judaism that have nothing to do with Zionism. In other words, Krem Miskevich is strikingly similar to the infamous "Soup Nazi" on the Seinfeld show. "No pierogi for you" because you're a Jew who supports Israel.

They claim that their refusal to serve me is based on who I have represented as a lawyer. That, of course, is the essence of McCarthyism. In other words, their defense against accusations of anti-Zionism is McCarthyism. I don't know which is worse!

Many residents of Martha's Vineyard have shown their support for my fight against bigotry, but a considerable number support the bigot. Not surprisingly, their refusal to sell to me increased their pierogi sales at the farmers market. There is a very strong anti-Israel component on Martha's Vineyard, as there is a strong element of hard-left radicalism. So I don't know whether the farmers market will adopt the rule I've asked them to adopt: namely, that in order to be a vendor at the farmers market one has to be willing to sell to everybody. I hope they will do that, but if not, this case may end up in the judicial system, which will have to decide whether Zionists are included in the class of people against whom discrimination is prohibited. Based on the close connection between Zionism and Judaism, they should be.

Chapter 7

Does the UN Do More Harm Than Good?

I recently went to the United Nations to watch Israeli Prime Minister Benjamin Netanyahu give his annual speech to the general assembly. What I saw before the speech even began has persuaded me that the United Nations is no longer merely on life support — it's clinically dead.

More than half of the delegates to the general assembly walked out the moment Netanyahu was introduced, refusing to listen to Israel's side of the contested narrative regarding the Middle East conflict. If the United Nations has one legitimate function, it's certainly to encourage the exchange of views regarding conflicts. But most of its member nations refuse even to listen to Israel. Some of them don't even recognize Israel's legitimate existence as the nation-state of the Jewish people. Many of these same countries that don't recognize Israel, do recognize the nonexistent state of "Palestine." There's nothing logically or historically inconsistent with these positions, since many of the countries that recognize

Palestine do so in order to deny recognition to Israel. There is actually very little support for a two-state solution at the general assembly. Most of those who support Palestine support it as an *alternative* to Israel, rather than as a country that could live in peace alongside the nation-state of the Jewish people.

Recall that virtually all the nations that walked out on Israel have listened to and cheered some of the most antidemocratic and barbarous regimes in the world including Iran, Sudan, Russia, Belarus, Cuba, China, and Venezuela. Many would cheer Hamas. Some would probably cheer Hitler. But Israel and its prime minister? No way will they even sit respectfully and listen.

Nor was the mass walkout merely a protest against Israel's war in Gaza. Many of these countries routinely walked out on Israel before the Gaza war began. I know, because I have been coming to the Netanyahu speech since he became prime minister. This most recent walkout was more extensive but many who participated would likely continue to walk out even if the Gaza war were to end. Moreover, there are other ways to protest particular polices than by refusing to listen to arguments. There can be and have been resolutions condemning the war against Hamas.

What then is the use of the United Nations? It used to be called a meaningless debate society. Now it's not even that. Debate requires listening to all sides of disputes. Debate can't be conducted when most of the audience refuses to hear one side. That's how it is at the United Nations.

What happened on September 26, 2025 is only an overt demonstration of what has long been true but covert. In the 1960s, Israel's representative to the United Nations, Abba Eban, quipped that if Algeria presented a resolution that the world was flat and Israel flattened it, it would pass by a vote of 112 to 17 with 35 abstentions. He could even identify each country's vote before there was any debate.

The only difference is that back in the 1960s, Israel's enemies would *pretend* to be considering all sides of the issue. Now, there's not even a pretense.

So what good does the United Nations now do? And if it does some good—which is highly questionable—does the evil outweigh that minimal good?

I'm not talking about some of the specialized agencies that deal with aviation, environment, and health. They can continue to exist independently, even if the United Nations were to be shut down. Just as the useful organs of dead bodies can be transplanted to live bodies, so too the useful agencies that are currently part of the UN can be transplanted to international bodies that do good. Other current UN agencies, such as those dealing with refugees, human rights, and justice contribute to the ills of the world rather than solving them. They should be abolished or transformed.

All in all, what started out as a wonderful experiment in international peacekeeping has turned into a source of bigotry, an incubator for antisemitism, and an expensive do-nothing organization that does more harm than good even when it actually tries to do something.

I was a big supporter of the United Nations as a young person. I consulted with our representative to the United Nations, Arthur Goldberg, following the 1967 Middle East war (the Six-Day War) when the security council unanimously approved a resolution designed to end the conflict. Isael accepted that resolution. All the Arab states rejected it.

Watching these bigoted delegates representing hypocritical nations around the world walk out *only* on the world's *only* nation-state of the Jewish people is the straw that has changed my view about whether the United States should continue its membership in and support of this organization.

I now believe the United States does not belong in the United Nations, for the same reason it doesn't belong to the international court of justice. I would not be unhappy if it closed down the monument to bigotry that I can see outside of my window in New York. I support the legislation proposed by Senator Lee, R-Utah, to get the US out of the UN and to get the UN out of the US.

Chapter 8

Zohran Mamdani's Threat to Arrest Prime Minister Benjamin Netanyahu— Nothing but Grandstanding

Is mayoral candidate Zohran Mamdani serious when he talks about arresting Prime Minister Benjamin Netanyahu next time he visits New York City—or is this just silly grandstanding designed to win applause from radical anti-Israel zealots?

Even if Mamdani wanted to follow through, the idea collapses on contact with reality. Is he planning to dispatch the NYPD to handcuff Netanyahu at JFK airport—while he's protected by the Secret Service and Mossad? Will a local judge issue a warrant and expect Netanyahu to self-surrender at One Police Plaza? Does he imagine Police Commissioner Jessica Tisch, a vocal supporter of Israel, would carry it out?

And then there's the law. Under US law, sitting heads of state enjoy diplomatic immunity. Arresting Netanyahu would violate that immunity and immediately trigger federal intervention. Foreign policy isn't made at Gracie Mansion—it's the prerogative of the White House.

When it comes to the International Criminal Court (ICC), the US position has been consistent for decades. Neither the US nor Israel ever joined the court, and presidents from both parties have dismissed it as unaccountable, politicized, and a threat to sovereignty. In 2002, Congress went further by passing the American Servicemembers' Protection Act—nicknamed the "Invade the Hague Act"—which flatly prohibits state and local officials from helping the ICC target US personnel or leaders of allied nations. The only narrow exceptions allow federal action against America's enemies, such as Saddam Hussein or Osama bin Laden. They do not cover allies like Israel—and they certainly don't empower a New York mayor to freelance foreign policy.

Even the ICC's own rules undermine this warrant. Under the Rome Statute's complementarity principle, the court can intervene only when a country is "unwilling or unable" to hold its leaders accountable. Israel, with its active and independent judiciary—a judiciary that has convicted and imprisoned a past prime minister and a past president—hardly qualifies.

And the charges themselves don't withstand factual scrutiny. The ICC arrest warrant accuses Netanyahu of intentionally starving civilians in Gaza. Yet, since the start of the war, Israel has facilitated the delivery of more than a million tons of food into Gaza—all while fighting Hamas, the very group that carried out mass murder, kidnappings, and rape on October 7. To call this "a crime against humanity" ignores both the facts and the unprecedented reality of a country supplying humanitarian aid to people living under the control of its attackers, even if the ICC didn't accuse Netanyahu of "genocide," as mistakenly alleged by Mamdani.

The arrest warrant in this case was not grounded in facts or law but politics. ICC Prosecutor Karim Khan issued the warrant against Netanyahu immediately upon learning that he faced credible allegations of sexual misconduct, using the warrant as a diversion. Khan planned to travel to Israel to conduct an investigation. I know, because I arranged the trip with his deputy. But he canceled it upon learning of the sex allegations and issued the warrants. That history prompted US sanctions against him. Yet Mamdani seems to ignore this important context and would have New York play along.

Should a Mayor Mamdani still attempt such a stunt, I would represent Netanyahu—as I have done in the past with regard to the ICC—and sue Mamdani under all applicable federal law. It would be the easiest win of my career.

Mamdani's pledge to arrest Netanyahu is not only misguided— it is reckless. New Yorkers deserve leaders focused on the city's real challenges, not grandstanding gestures that flirt with illegality and embarrass this great city on the world stage.

If Mamdani's threat is meant as a political statement, it is one that risks serious consequences—with no chance of legal success, though it may earn him the votes of the increasing number of anti-Israel New Yorkers. If it is meant as a serious promise that he would try to arrest Netanyahu, then bring it on!

Conclusion

Trump's Peace Plan Succeeds Because of Israel's Military Victories

President Trump's brilliant diplomacy has resulted in freeing the hostages and implementing a cease-fire. If the truce persists, it will be a great accomplishment and an important step toward peace—if only a cold peace—in the region. It might also provide a stepping-stone to a more enduring and somewhat warmer peace. Mr. Trump deserves enormous credit for his role in putting together a coalition of Arab and Muslim states and in pressuring both sides to accept what they each understandably regard as compromises.

It is important to note, though, that Israel's decisive military victories in Gaza, Lebanon, Syria, and Iran were the essential pre-requisite to Mr. Trump's accomplishments. These victories, which were extremely costly to both sides in human lives, made it possible to pressure Hamas to accept an agreement that many Hamas supporters regard as near suicidal to the organization.

Because of Israel's spectacular military accomplishments, Hamas lost the support of its major allies, especially Hezbollah, Syria, and Iran. It was also in the process of losing support among

Palestinians, particularly in Gaza, because of the enormous toll the war, started by Hamas, exacted from civilians. Without Israel's military successes combined with Mr. Trump's diplomatic pressures, Hamas would still be fighting, the hostages would still be in Gaza tunnels, and there would be more bloodshed and death on both sides.

Had Israel followed the terrible advice it was offered by the Biden administration, by the *New York Times*'s opinion pages (including the nearly always-wrong Thomas Friedman), by American left-wing academics, by CNN pundits, and by others who counseled "restraint," Israel would not have entered Rafah. It would not have killed Hamas leaders.

Israel, too, would have abandoned the Philadelphi Corridor; it would never have bombed Iranian nuclear facilities; it would not have aggressively gone after Hezbollah and other Iranian surrogates in the region, and it would have agreed to a cease-fire on disadvantageous terms.

Even if it had followed this awful advice, the anti-Israel and antisemitic demonstrations around the world would not have diminished, because they were not designed to help Palestinians, but rather to hurt the nation-state of the Jewish people. Israel was wise to ignore the ignorant and bigoted condemnation and name calling that it has endured since October 7. It was wise to focus on the only thing its enemies in the Middle East understand, and that is victory through strength.

Israel's enemies had to be convinced that the Israeli blood that was shed on October 7 was not cheap and that future attempts to shed Jewish blood—whether in the Middle East or around the world—will be responded to disproportionately. The message Israel has sent is that for every Israeli life that is taken by terrorists, multiple terrorists' lives will be taken, even if that requires some collateral damage to non-terrorists who support or cheer on the terrorism.

This justly disproportionate payback will not be deterred by these terrorists hiding behind human shields. Nor will it be deterred by fear of bigoted and one-sided condemnation of Israel by antisemites. Whatever legitimate criticisms that may have been directed at Israel's overreactions were drowned out by the illegitimate condemnation of Israel for doing what every democracy would do and has done.

The only response terrorists understand is making them pay a disproportionately heavy price for endangering Israeli life. Hamas leaders have threatened to repeat October 7, over and over again. Israel has counter-threatened that if they try to repeat October 7, Israel will repeat the two years that followed it, including the targeting of their leaders, wherever they are.

Deterrence through disproportionately overwhelming strength is the only way the Jewish state can live in peace and safety. It is also the only way other Arab and Muslim nations will consider making real peace and joining the Abraham Accords.

This reality—and its corollary that weakness produces aggression and death—has been proven over and over again through the millennia. As the Psalmist wrote: "God will give his people strength." And then: "God will bless his people with peace."

This self-evident truth was proven once again when Mr. Trump was able to bring about peace following demonstrated overwhelming strength by Israel and America. This peace will endure only as long as this overpowering strength endures, along with a willingness to use it when necessary.

Appendix

Much of this book, and my other writing about the Middle East, deal with language and morality. The misuse of powerful words such as "genocide" and "starvation" is intended to make moral points. In this appendix, published originally with extensive footnotes for a law review, I explore the relationship among language, law and morality.

The Relationship Among Language, Morality, and Law: The Chicken and the Egg

Which came first: language, morality, or law? The relationship among these three components of civilization is complex and ever-changing, with each influencing the other in subtle ways.

Law is based on language. Law's commands—its prohibitions, duties, punishments, and rewards—are all expressed in words. Often these words are inadequate to reflect the nuances of the moral underpinnings of the legal rules.

As Justice Oliver Wendell Holmes Jr. put it: "A word is not a crystal, transparent and unchanged, it is the skin of a living thought and may vary greatly in color and content according to the circumstances and time in which it is used." <u>Towne v. Eisner</u>, 245 U.S. 418, 425, 38 S. Ct. 158, 159, 62 L. Ed. 372 (1918). Because of the inherent inadequacy of language to capture the complexity of human thought and action, the law is often a blunderbuss, rather than a scalpel. Where morality suggests a continuum, the law demands arbitrary lines—on-off switches rather than dimmers. The result is often retail injustice at the edges in order to bring about wholesale justice at the core.

As Aristotle cautioned: "The law is always a general statement, yet there are cases which it is not possible to cover in a general statement. In matters therefore where, while it is necessary to speak in general terms, it is not possible to do so correctly, the law takes into consideration the majority of cases, although it is not unaware of the error this involves. And this does not make it a wrong law; for the error is not in the law nor the lawgiver, but in the nature of the case: the material of conduct is essentially irregular." Aristotle, Nicomachean Ethics.

There are those who argue that human beings are naturally endowed not only with a grammar of language, but also with a universal grammar of morality. If this were true, it would also suggest a universal language of law, since morality and law are so closely connected. Indeed, some degrees and types of morality may well have preceded language.

Evidence suggests some degree of universality in the <u>language</u> employed by morality and law—at least at the most abstract level. Concepts such as fairness, due process, equality, property, evidence, guilt, justification, and excuse seem pervasive, though in varying degrees, in nearly all systems of law and morality. But this commonality of <u>language</u> often masks real differences in the law and morality <u>in action</u>. The Constitution of the Soviet Union was a model of rights and liberties!

The American Declaration of Independence spoke of equality—"all men are created equal"—at a time when slavery was central to the economies not only of the South but also of the North, and Black "men" were considered "property" that their white owners had a "right" to possess, exploit, and sell.

Yet the language of equality played an important role in the formation of our nation. The same can be said about many other nations, including Israel, whose founding documents employed the language of equality, but whose actions—perhaps born of necessity—often were at variance with that language.

Language often reflects aspirations, rather than reality. It forces citizens to acknowledge the hypocrisy represented by the disparity between words and deeds. If hypocrisy is the "homage vice pays to virtue" as Rochefoucauld once observed, then it is important to maintain the language of aspiration as we engage in the never-ending struggle to move ignoble deeds closer to noble words.

The "chicken-egg" question inevitably arises in considering the relationship among language, law, and morality and which comes first. John tells us that "in the beginning was the word," but anthropology teaches that the deed preceded the word—that there was killing before there was a prohibition against killing, as the biblical story of Cain exemplifies. Only after his murder of Abel did the Bible ordain that he "who sheddeth man's blood, by man shall his blood be shed." (Genesis 9:6). Freud also placed the deed before the word when he quipped that when the first man who "flung a word of abuse at his enemy instead of a spear was the founder of civilization."

Does the language of a particular culture influence its morality and law? Or does the morality and law of a particular culture influence its language? Both are obviously true to some degree.

The word "right," for example, is not common in early, religion-based cultures. It becomes more common as cultures move toward democracy and recognize that individuals are entitled to have certain expectations in relationship to the government.[2]

Words matter. Language is a weapon of advocacy. As President John Kennedy said of Churchill: "[H]e mobilized the English language and sent it into battle." Evil leaders such as Hitler have also mobilized their languages of hate. Many years ago, when I was a law clerk for Justice Arthur Goldberg, who had been America's most prominent labor lawyer, he gave me an example of the power of language. Organized labor was fighting for a provision that would require all workers in particular industries to join the union. Management was opposed to this provision.

The controversy was hot and heavy until management came up with a phrase describing their position as "the right to work." They sought "right to work laws." Goldberg told me that as soon as they came up with that phrase, the fight was over, since all Americans support the right to work. Similarly, when anti-abortionists came up with the phrase "right to life," they strengthened their position enormously, since the right to life trumped the right to choose in the minds of many undecided voters. Moreover, describing the fetus as a "baby" also substituted a powerful emotional word for an antiseptic scientific one. Other phrases—such as "the right to bear arms" and "victims' rights"—have also resonated with the public. Words really do matter.

In a rights-oriented society, bestowing the imprimatur of

---

2 "Right" has multiple meaning in current usage. In addition to legal entitlement, it also means "correct," as in "right and wrong," as well as "conservative," as in "right-wing." See "Law" in 8 Oxford English Dictionary (J. A. Simpson & E. S. C. Weiner, eds.) (2d. ed., 1989). There is no precise Biblical or ancient Hebrew word for rights (as we use the term today) because in most ancient legal cultures group obligations preceded individualistic notions of rights by many centuries. The Hebrew word for rights, *zchut*, derives from the ancient word for property or assets.

"righthood" on a preference or a power changes the nature of the debate. This has been true as far back as when kings claimed the "divine right" of monarchs, even though the word "right" had no real meaning in the context of such a claim, since rights, properly understood, are claims against the power of the government. Likewise, the emotive phrase "victims' rights" makes little rational sense, especially in the context of the criminal justice system, since the government is on the side of the victims. Thus, the term "victims' rights" has been used, essentially, to deny criminal defendants their constitutional rights to which they are entitled when prosecuted by the government.

There are other ways as well in which language influences law and morality. Consider the word "law" itself. In the English language, the word "law" has several distinctive meanings: it means the ever-changing human-made law, such as the Internal Revenue Code, the Penal Code, and the Constitution; but it also means the immutable laws of nature, such as Newton's laws of gravity, the laws of physics, and Einstein's laws of relativity; and for some it means the "natural law" of God (or some other objective or external source) that trumps positive, man-made law.[3] In other languages, there are

---

3 In the sciences, the word "law" is also used in describing "a theoretical principle deduced from particular facts . . . and expressible by the statement that a particular phenomenon always occurs if certain conditions be present." The word "law" in this scientific sense was first used in the 17th century by Johannes Kepler in his *New Astronomy* (1609). It was later also used by Galilei, Descartes, Leibniz, and Newton. In the physical sciences, those laws are also sometimes called "law of nature" and "natural law" because they were viewed "as commands imposed by the Deity upon matter." Even writers who did not accept this view, like Spinoza, often spoke of them as "obeyed" by the phenomena, or as "agents by which the phenomena are produced." *See* Oxford English Dictionary, *supra note 9*, at 714. Other languages, too, use their word for "law" in the scientific

distinct words for these very different types of "law" (as in some
cold cultures there are numerous words for different kinds of snow).
This trichotomy of American usage regarding the loaded word
"law" sometimes confuses students and may incline some toward
an unthinking acceptance of the concept of "natural law," that is
prescriptive rules of conduct that are as immutable and external as
the "laws" of physics.

Most languages have two terms for law—one refers to law that
derives its authority from the power of the legislature; the other
refers to a broader sense of law, encompassing not only statutory law
but eternal principles of justice. The fact that the English language
does not make this distinction between ius and lex (in Latin) or
Recht and Gesetz (in German) causes not only confusion but may
have wide-ranging implications. For instance, the legal philosopher
H.L.A. Hart argued that that having two notions allows courts
to deal with crimes which were committed in perfectly legal form
under an earlier regime. So, German courts in the 1950s could
rebut the Eichmann defense—that one was just following orders—by
declaring, "This may have been the Gesetz but it certainly was not
Recht."

Some scholars also argue that the lack of systematic ambiguity in the English language when using the word "law" results in
an imprecision when the concept of "the rule of law" is invoked:
does an English speaker mean a Gesetzesstaat—a state based on laws

---

context. In German, for instance, a *Naturgesetz* can describe physical laws,
such as Newton's law. But *Naturgesetz* can also mean *natural law* in the
jurisprudential sense, as in "the natural law theory of Aquinas." In other
words, it can have a descriptive and normative meaning. "*Naturgesetz*,"
in *UTB Handwoerterbuch der Philosophie* [Dictionary of Philosophy]. The
same is true for the French word *loi naturelle*. "Loi naturelle," in Linternaute
Encylopedie, available at http://www.linternaute.com/dictionnaire/fr
/definition/loi-naturelle.

laid down—or Rechtsstaat—a state committed to higher principles of justice?

Language has power that can cut both ways. Consider the word "rape." In its original meaning, rape conveyed a sense of force, violence, and physical brutality. The image of the rapist was the stranger who physically assaulted his victim in a dark alley either by grabbing her from behind and forcing himself on her, or by threatening to kill her with a gun or knife. Over time, the meaning of rape has been expanded to include date rape that involved a lack of consent without force or threat of violence, and even rape by "fraud" or "trickery."[4] This may be a positive development, but it has diluted the power of the word "rape," so that today the image of the "rapist" includes the drunken college freshman who doesn't believe that "no"—or the absence of "yes"—now means "no," both as a matter of law and morality.

It is fair to ask whether it would have been better, all things considered, to maintain the original connotation of the word "rape" and to employ different words—such as "unconsented to sex," or "sex by fraud"—to define new crimes representing the emerging approach to sexual autonomy and the requirement of affirmative and knowing consent. Reasonable people can and do disagree about this. The important point is that there are consequences—some positive, some negative—to expanding (and diluting) the meaning of a powerful word such as "rape."

The same is true of terms like racism, anti-Semitism, homophobia, sexism, and Islamophobia. These once powerful words of conscription have been softened in their impact by their political weaponization and promiscuous invocation. Language influences law

---

4 In addition, the word "rape" is used to describe factually "consensual" sex with an underage person—often sixteen or seventeen—who is deemed by law to be incapable of legal consent.

and morality in myriad ways. Consider, for example, the way in which the literary narrative influences the way we look at crime. The classic literary narrative, like the Biblical narrative, is logical, coherent, and purposive. Chekhov put it aptly when he advised a young playwright that "[i]f in the first chapter you say that a gun hung on the wall, in the second, or third chapter it must without fail be discharged." In literature, as in the Bible, there is no coincidence, randomness, or superfluous in the use of language. Every word or act has a raison d'être—a role in the narrative, a purpose. In real life, to the contrary, most words and acts are purposeless, random, and without meaning.[5] Many literary, biblical, and even constitutional scholars live by a rule of teleology that has little resonance in real life—namely, that every event, character, and word has a purpose. "To every thing there is a season, and a time to every purpose under heaven," says Ecclesiastes. God does not engage in redundancy, say the Talmudists. Freud, whose forebears came from that tradition, similarly believed that all words, even those dreamed or spoken in error, have meaning. Some lawyers who view our Constitution in near biblical terms—and who seek to discern the true meaning of those near deities who wrote it—fall into the same teleo-/theological trap: every word of that secularly sacred text must have a purpose, a meaning, and if we only had the wisdom of the framers, we could discern it.

But life does not imitate art. Life is not a purposive narrative that follows Chekhov's canon. Words and events are often simply meaningless, irrelevant to what comes next; in real life, our words and actions can be out of sequence, random, purely accidental, without purpose. If our universe and its inhabitants are governed by

---

5 *See* Alan M. Dershowitz, "Life Is Not a Dramatic Narrative," in Peter Brooks & Paul Gewirtz (Eds.), *Law's Stories: Narrative and Rhetoric in the Law* 99 (1996).

rules of chaos, randomness, and purposelessness, then many of the stories—if they can even be called stories—will often lack meaning. Human beings always try to impose order and meaning on random chaos, both to understand and to control the forces that determine their destiny. This desperate attempt to derive purpose from purposelessness will often distort reality, as, indeed, Chekhov's canon surely does.

In Chekhovian drama, chest pains are followed by heart attacks, coughs by consumption, life insurance policies by murders, telephone rings by dramatic messages. In real life, most chest pains are indigestion, coughs are colds, insurance policies are followed by years of premium payments, and telephone calls are from marketing services.

To be sure, after the fact, we may be able to offer a plausible retrospective account, a story, or a narrative. As Sartre put it: "When you tell about life. . .[y]ou seen to start at the beginning. . . And in reality you have started at the end."[6] Narrative often starts at the end. But rarely can we employ such retrospective accounts to predict their reoccurrence. Nor is the lack of prophetic ability merely a function of our relative ignorance. Often it is simply in the nature of things.

Quantum physics corroborates on the micro level what paleontology teaches on the macro level. The most important rule in the game of life is that generally there are no knowable rules.

Perhaps it is the often-unspoken recognition of this nihilistic reality that drives us so powerfully toward perspective human laws by which we can exercise some control over our mostly random destiny and toward purposive narratives by which we seek to impose an order on the largely disordered words and deeds of life.

---

6 Jean-Paul Sartre, *Nausea*, 57 (New Directions, 2007) [1938].

This critical dichotomy between teleological rules of drama, on the one hand, and the mostly random rules of real life, on the other, has profoundly important implications for our legal system. When we import the narrative form of storytelling into our legal system—when we rearrange words to create a coherent narrative—we confuse fiction with fact and endanger the truth-finding function of the adjudicative process. Fact finders are familiar with the dramatic form—not only from Chekhov but also from pulp novels, mysteries, movies, and television shows. They expect a beginning, a middle, and an end to each story. In drama, life unfolds in acts or chapters or between commercials. There is an internal logic to the structure. Defense attorneys now use this expectation to try to persuade jurors that there must be a reasonable doubt, if there are any loose ends to the prosecutor's narration. This is called the "law and order" tactic, named after the popular TV show. Life, as actually lived, is filled with randomness.

I once used this insight to win an appeal involving a businessman who had taken out a life insurance policy on his partner ten days before the partner was gunned down by a professional hit man. The District Attorney persuaded the jury that the timing could not possibly be coincidental and the businessman was convicted. I argued that the appellate court should not look at the case as if it were a made-for-TV movie, but rather as a slice of real life, full of irrelevant actions and coincidences. I asked the judges how many of them had taken out life insurance on a loved one and what their neighbors would have thought if that loved one had died shortly thereafter. The court agreed and reversed the conviction.

Among the most pervasive narratives in the human experience have been the stories of justice. In these stories, virtue is rewarded, vice punished, and justice achieved. The Psalmist reports, "I have been young, and now am old; yet have I not seen the righteous forsaken, nor his seed begging bread." This is a narrative of justice.

But it is a perversely false narrative. It is false because the history of humankind is replete with the abandonment of the righteous and their children. It is perverse because it implies that those who are abandoned must necessarily have been unrighteous. In the early days of the motion picture industry, the Hays Commission required all films to follow this false heuristic, so as to persuade viewers that we live in a just world that does not require change. A Jewish commentator once used the absence of justice here on earth as an argument for a heaven in which early injustices are remedied.

The great Israeli novelist Amos Oz contrasted the Shakespearean and Chekhovian dramatic narratives in the context of the Middle East conflict:

> At the end of a Shakespearean tragedy, the stage is strewn with dead bodies and maybe there's some justice hovering high above. A Chekhov tragedy, on the other hand, ends with everybody disillusioned, embittered, heartbroken, disappointed, absolutely shattered, but still alive. And I want a Chekhovian resolution, not a Shakespearean one, for the Israeli-Palestinian tragedy.[7]

In real life, as distinguished from dramatic narrative, the resolution, if there ever is one, is likelier to be even messier than in Chekhov's plays.

To paraphrase Holmes, the life of the law should not be

---

7 Quoted in Johann Hari, "A Life in Focus, Amos Oz, Israeli Literary Colossus and Lifelong Advocate of A Two-State Solution," *The Independent*, Dec. 31, 2018, available at https://www.the-independent .com/news/obituaries/amoz-oz-dead-israeli-writer-novelist-palestine-israel -tale-of-love-and-darkness-a8705681.html (reprinting an interview from 2009).

teleo-logic or theo-logic (neither of which is logic at all); it should be human experience. And human experience cannot be cabined into the structure of narrative, language or words. Let the language of literature continue to borrow from law and life (though it would borrow more accurately if it looked less to Chekhov for its canons of structure and more to Proust, Kerouac, and Mamet). But let law develop its own rules of language, grammar structure, and editing—of evidence, relevance, and prejudice—by looking to the vagaries of real human experience.[8] And let fact finders be warned that life is not a Shakespearean or Chekhovian narrative.

Language, even in the hands and pens of its greatest practitioners, will never be capable of probing all the nuances of the human condition. Even Shakespeare and Dostoyevsky, whose insights into the inner workings of the human psyche and soul are unparalleled, recognized that the language of the law, in its feeble efforts to reflect the human condition, is an inadequate mirror of life. But language is all we have to communicate experience from generation to generation, and without this capacity to transmit the knowledge acquired by one generation to another, humans would remain static, subject to only long-term evolution, as are all other animals, whose experiences gained over their lifetime die with them. Despite its limitations, language is what separates us from other species, and it is what makes law possible.

---

8   Of course, human experience is itself distorted by one's interpretation of past events, which, in turn, is driven by men's need to create a narrative around random, independent events. *See, e.g.*, Daniel Kahneman, *Thinking, Fast and Slow*, Ch. 19 (2011).